W9-BIS-995

Residential Mortgage Banking Basics

REAL ESTATE FINANCE PRESS

MBA

Published by the
Mortgage Bankers Association of America
1919 Pennsylvania Ave., N.W.
Washington, D.C. 20006

Copyright © 1998 by the Mortgage Bankers Association of America. All rights reserved. No part of this publication may be reproduced in any form by any means without the prior written permission of the MBA.

Foreword and Acknowledgments

Residential Mortgage Banking Basics is produced by the Education department of the Mortgage Bankers Association of America to provide mortgage bankers, as well as other real estate finance professionals, a concise introduction to the business of mortgage banking and the functions comprising the mortgage lending process. Credit goes to Lynn S. Powell for writing the original text.

Special thanks to William H. Brewster, who edited and updated the text for this edition. Mr. Brewster is Vice President and Manager of Policies & Compliance at Columbia National, Incorporated, an independent residential and commercial mortgage banker with headquarters in Columbia, Maryland. He is a former Assistant Director of Government Agency Relations at the Mortgage Bankers Association of America in Washington, DC, and residential loan originator in the Baltimore-Washington area. He holds B.A. and M.A. degrees from the State University of New York at Albany.

Table of Contents   Page

INTRODUCTION TO MORTGAGE BANKING 1

OVERVIEW OF THE MORTGAGE BANKING PROCESS . . . 1

MORTGAGE BANKING REVENUE 3

TYPES OF MORTGAGE SPECIALISTS 4

MORTGAGE LOAN TYPES 4

PARTICIPANTS IN THE MORTGAGE BANKING INDUSTRY . . 6

SECONDARY MARKETING 9

PRIMARY AND SECONDARY MORTGAGE MARKETS . . . 9

SELLING IN THE SECONDARY MARKET 10

    Whole Loan Sales 10

    Participation Loan Sales 11

    Mortgage-Backed Security Sales 11

    Managing the Pipeline 11

    Investor Commitments 11

    Pricing 12

RISK MANAGEMENT 12

LOAN ORIGINATION 15

GENERATING MORTGAGE BANKING BUSINESS 15

QUALITIES AND RESPONSIBILITIES
    OF THE LOAN ORIGINATOR 16

MORTGAGE BANKING LOAN PROGRAMS 17

COMPLETION OF THE LOAN APPLICATION 19

REGULATORY COMPLIANCE 20

APPLICATION FOLLOW-UP 21

LOAN PROCESSING 23

LOAN FILE SETUP 23

PROCESSING DIFFERENT LOAN TYPES 25

FHA Loans 25

VA Loans 25

FmHA Loans 26

Conventional Loans 26

UNDERWRITING 27

QUALITIES AND RESPONSIBILITIES OF
THE UNDERWRITER 27

FOUR "Cs" OF UNDERWRITING 28

THE UNDERWRITING DECISION 30

LOAN CLOSING 31

PREPARING AND ASSEMBLING CLOSING DOCUMENTS . . 31

FUNDING THE MORTGAGE LOAN 33

RECORDING THE MORTGAGE DOCUMENTS 34

MORTGAGE WAREHOUSING 35

WAREHOUSE LINES OF CREDIT 35

INTEREST RATES, FEES AND COMPENSATING BALANCES . 36

WAREHOUSE SPREAD 36

COLLATERAL 36

REQUIRED DOCUMENTATION 37

ALTERNATIVES TO WAREHOUSING 37

SHIPPING AND DELIVERY 39

INVESTOR COMMITMENTS 40

SHIPPING DUTIES 40

LOAN ADMINISTRATION 43

LOAN ADMINISTRATION INCOME 44

SERVICING AGREEMENT 44

LOAN FILE SETUP 45

MORTGAGE LOAN PAYMENTS 45

ESCROWS 45

CUSTOMER SERVICE 46

INVESTOR ACCOUNTING 46

DELINQUENCIES AND FORECLOSURES 46

INTRODUCTION TO MORTGAGE BANKING

1

What is residential mortgage banking? Residential mortgage banking is the origination, sale and servicing of mortgage loans secured by residential real estate. The term "mortgage banking" is somewhat misleading. It implies that mortgage banking is funded or capitalized by customer deposits, as are banks and thrifts. In reality, mortgage bankers are financial intermediaries that facilitate mortgage transactions. They fund operations with short-term capital borrowings, usually from commercial banks.

For borrowers, mortgage bankers originate the mortgage loans that allow them to purchase real estate. For investors, mortgage bankers provide investment opportunities by selling the loans they originate. This process of originating and selling mortgage loans moves capital from surplus to deficit regions. Thus it maintains an even geographic distribution of available mortgage money for housing and commercial development.

Residential mortgage lending is production-oriented, and operates at its peak with a high-volume, continuous flow of loans being originated, marketed and serviced. Documentation and procedures are standardized. Per loan profits are low, but processing and loan administration activities are usually automated — allowing economies of scale to boost profits from operations. Cash flows are predictable, except to the extent they are affected by exposure to interest rate changes.

OVERVIEW OF THE MORTGAGE BANKING PROCESS

Essential to understanding "What is Mortgage Banking?" is the basic knowledge of the mortgage banking process — the steps in which mortgage loans are created, sold and serviced.

The process begins when, in the primary mortgage market, a mortgage banker makes long-term mortgage loans secured by real

1

estate. The loans are funded at closing by short-term lines of credit. Groups of closed loans are pooled together for sale to investors in the secondary mortgage market. The proceeds from the sale repay outstanding lines of credit and the cycle starts again.

The mortgage banking process is a complex series of interrelated activities. Each activity is conducted in accordance with specific investor requirements and government regulations. An explanation of the process begins with secondary marketing, since this activity controls the other mortgage banking activities.

- Secondary marketing is the sale of existing loans to investors, and management of the risk associated with mortgages. Normally the sale is arranged simultaneously with the origination of loans. Commitments are used to secure the future sale of loans and protect against interest rate changes that may occur between the dates of origination and sale.

- Origination is the creation of mortgages. Loan officers initiate the origination process by locating borrowers and making loan applications. The application records information about the borrower and the property to be mortgaged. It is supported by personal documents (W-2s, tax returns, bank statements, etc.) provided by the borrower.

- Processing is the collection of documentation and verifications to support information provided on the loan application. An appraisal is ordered to confirm the value of the mortgaged property and a credit report is obtained to disclose the borrower's credit history.

- Underwriting is the evaluation of loan documentation to approve or deny the loan. In the evaluation process, the underwriter considers specific requirements to be met to ensure a quality loan that is salable in the secondary mortgage market.

- Closing is the signing and recording of loan documentation, plus the disbursement of loan funds.

- Warehousing is the financing of loans from closing until sale to an investor. Short-term, revolving lines of credit are the most typical form of financing used by mortgage bankers.

- Shipping and delivery is the packaging of closed loan files for delivery to an investor. This consummates the loan sale.

- Loan administration is the collection, recordation and remittance of monthly mortgage payments to investors. Servicing also includes the maintenance of escrows to protect the property securing each loan.

Profitable mortgage banking operations require effective communication and teamwork among all departments. Mortgage banking staff involved in each lending activity must be aware of the types, volume and delivery timing of mortgage products being committed for sale by marketing. This ensures the mortgage banking process will occur in harmony.

MORTGAGE BANKING REVENUE

Mortgage bankers generate income through:

- origination fees,

- warehouse spread,

- secondary market sales and

- service fees.

Origination fees are paid by borrowers to lenders to cover costs associated with originating loans. These fees are applied against lender overhead, which includes personnel, document preparation, lender inspections, underwriter review, warehouse fees and other expenses. Origination expenses usually exceed origination fees. The loan origination fee is stated as a percentage of the original loan amount, usually 1 percent. The amounts of separate ancillary fees will vary by loan type and state. Fees to pay third parties, such as those for appraisal and credit report, are also collected on a typical transaction.

Warehouse spread is the difference between the interest rate being paid on the lender's short-term credit line and the interest being received by the lender on the mortgages funded by the credit line. While the interest rate differential is small, the balance of the credit line outstanding is quite large and can result in considerable income for the mortgage banker. The rate charged on the line of credit is adjusted downward for sizable tax and insurance escrow deposits. Therefore, the larger the deposits, the lower the warehouse rate and the greater the warehouse spread.

Secondary market income comes from the sale of mortgages to investors in the secondary market. If the loans can be sold at a price greater than the price at the time of origination, the mortgage banker realizes income. Since prices vary with interest rates, commitments are used to lock in prices. Commitments generally have the effect of keeping marketing revenue-neutral in most interest rate environments.

Loan administration is where mortgage bankers derive their greatest income. Here, economies of scale allow servicing personnel to conduct efficient, profitable operations with relatively large servicing portfolios. The mortgage banker receives a fee, typically between 25 and 44 basis points of a loan's outstanding principal per year, to perform the collection and remittance functions associated with servicing. Servicing also provides the opportunity for mortgage bankers to provide related services (insurance, consumer loans, etc.) and collect related fees (late payment penalties, assumption fees, etc.).

TYPES OF MORTGAGE SPECIALISTS

Mortgage lending relies on a variety of specialists. "Full-service" mortgage bankers can perform every activity in the mortgage banking process. They often service loans after the loans are sold to an investor. Loan administration (also known as "servicing") consists of collecting monthly loan payments, forwarding loan proceeds to investors who have purchased the loans, maintaining escrow accounts for the payment of taxes and insurance, and acting as the investors' representative if any problems arise with the loans. In recent years, mortgage bankers have become increasingly specialized, becoming proficient in specific niche areas of real estate finance.

Mortgage brokers bring borrowers and lenders together to create new loans, or bring lenders and investors together to sell existing loans. They specialize in origination.

Correspondents specialize in the origination and processing of loans. Correspondents may or may not underwrite new mortgages, depending on who the recipient of the loans will be. Newly originated loans are sold, along with servicing rights, to banks, thrifts or wholesale mortgage lenders.

The correspondent uses sales proceeds to fund additional origination. Profits are made through origination fees and gains realized from loan sales.

Wholesalers specialize in the purchase and servicing of mortgages obtained from other specialists, often correspondents or loan brokers. In some cases they underwrite, close and fund the loans they buy to add to their servicing portfolios. Other wholesalers buy closed loans, typically FHA and VA mortgages. Income in the wholesale business is derived from servicing fees and marketing gains on loan sales to investors.

Conduits specialize in the purchase of loans in the secondary market where they pool the loans for sale to investors as securities. Sales to investors in the secondary market are normally conducted through investment banking firms. Income is earned from marketing fees and secondary market sales.

MORTGAGE LOAN TYPES

Just as there are several types of mortgage bankers, there are several types of mortgage loan programs. The three predominant loan types are government insured (FHA loans), government-guaranteed (VA and FmHA loans) and conventional loans (loans without government backing).

The Federal Housing Administration (FHA) was created in 1934 and is today the division of the Department of Housing and

Urban Development (HUD) that administers the FHA loan program. FHA loans insure lenders against foreclosure losses on residential mortgages. This insurance lessens the risk assumed by lenders in making high-balance, low-down-payment loans at market rates of interest. To support the program, borrowers pay a mortgage insurance premium (MIP).

The Department of Veterans Affairs (VA) home loan guarantee program was created in 1944. VA guarantees, in the case of default, repayment to the lender of a specified percentage of each mortgage loan made to qualified veterans. This repayment is called entitlement. The veteran need not make a downpayment, but must pay a funding fee. The amount of this fee depends on a variety of factors, including whether the veteran makes a downpayment and whether the veteran has had a VA mortgage in the past. Although the federal government provides a guarantee, lenders typically still lose money on VA foreclosures.

The Department of Agriculture's Farmers Home Administration (FmHA) very recently began to offer housing guarantees to lenders who lend to qualified homebuyers in designated rural areas of the country. This program, administered by the Rural Housing and Community Development Service, provides a partial guarantee to eligible homebuyers, who in turn need make no downpayment. The

guarantee fee for this program is .9% of the mortgage amount. Maximum borrower income is restricted to a set percent of the median in each county.

Conventional loans generally carry no government insurance or guarantee. The loans are often secured by private mortgage insurance (MI) if the down payment is less than 20% of the value of the mortgaged property. Because there is generally no government backing, conventional loans normally require larger downpayments and carry higher interest rates than government loans.

In recent years, many special conventional loan programs have been created which specifically target first-time and underserved homebuyers. These special programs, many of them sponsored by state and local governmental agencies, often subsidize the downpayment, closing cost payment and/or interest rate. Like FHA and VA loans, these special conventional programs are generally limited by loan size. Unlike FHA and VA, they may also be limited by household income.

In addition to FHA, VA, FmHA and conventional loans, mortgages are also distinguished by their amortization and repayment patterns. The most common types are the fixed rate mortgage (FRM), the adjustable rate mortgage (ARM), the graduated payment mortgage (GPM), buydowns, two-steps and balloons.

PARTICIPANTS IN THE MORTGAGE BANKING INDUSTRY

Mortgage lending involves a variety of participants, vital to completing the mortgage banking process. They include:

- borrowers,

- lenders,

- government agencies,

- government-sponsored enterprises (GSEs),

- private agencies and

- investors.

Borrowers are consumers financing primary, secondary or investment residences. They can also be builders and developers financing residential subdivisions. Borrowers are usually matched with lenders via referrals from real estate agents, builders, mortgage brokers and other sources.

Lenders are mortgage bankers, commercial banks, mutual savings banks, savings and loan associations, credit unions and others capable of lending money for mortgages. These institutions may hold the mortgages they create in portfolio for investment purposes, or sell the mortgage into the secondary mortgage market.

Government agencies include those already mentioned — HUD, VA and the U.S. Department of Agriculture. HUD oversees both the FHA and the Government National Mortgage Association (GNMA or Ginnie Mae). Government agencies also include many state Housing Finance Agencies (HFAs), which, as already mentioned, administer state housing assistance programs that can work in tandem with other government and conventional programs.

In addition to facilitating the mortgage process, many federal and state government agencies regulate the operations of mortgage bankers. Even mortgage bankers that are owned independent of another financial institution are subject to strict governmental rules and limitations on advertising.

Government-sponsored enterprises (GSEs) include the Federal National Mortgage Association (FNMA or Fannie Mae) and the Federal Home Loan Mortgage Corporation (FHLMC or Freddie Mac). These GSEs and Ginnie Mae facilitate the secondary mortgage market by providing a network for the purchase, sale and guarantee of existing mortgages and mortgage pools. As a result, mortgage money to finance residential and commercial properties is available in every geographic region of the United States.

Private companies (other than lenders and investors) involved in mortgage lending include private mortgage insurers and private conduits. Mortgage insurers protect lenders against loan default by insuring high-balance loans (above 80% loan-to-value). Private conduits facilitate the secondary mortgage market by purchasing loans from lenders. These loans are pooled to form mortgage-backed securities and are sold to investors either directly or through investment bankers.

Investors purchase mortgages and mortgage-backed securities for investment purposes. These organizations invest large sums of money in long-term instruments. The most common private investors are life insurance companies and pension funds. GSEs and Ginnie Mae are sometimes called investors because they purchase mortgages as well as perform other duties.

These participants are involved in the mortgage banking process from origination to the sale of a mortgage. Each group has special interests and requirements that make mortgage transactions profitable. The remaining chapters will define and clarify the roles of these industry participants in the production, sale and servicing of mortgage loans.

SECONDARY MARKETING   2

Several common words have meanings unique to the mortgage banking industry. Marketing is one of those words. In mortgage banking, marketing has little to do with advertising or promoting products. Instead, marketing or secondary marketing is the sale of existing loans to investors and the management of risk associated with those loans.

Secondary marketing begins the mortgage banking process by committing loans for sale to investors. In some cases, the loans have not yet been originated. In other cases, the loans may be in process or "in the pipeline." Since marketing determines what loan products are to be originated, at what price, and when they are to be delivered to investors, it is not surprising that marketing controls production, underwriting, closing, warehousing, shipping and delivery activities.

Secondary marketing functions include:

- managing the pipeline,

- negotiating investor commitments,

- monitoring and establishing market prices,

- managing marketing risks and

- hedging.

PRIMARY AND SECONDARY MORTGAGE MARKETS

The primary mortgage market is where new loans are created. Borrowers seeking mortgage credit to finance real estate come to mortgage lenders who provide long-term funds with fixed and variable rates of interest.

The secondary mortgage market is where mortgage bankers and investors buy and sell existing and prospective loans. The secondary mortgage market provides liquidity to mortgages as investments, which allows mortgage bankers to meet immediate needs for capital and enables investors to invest in mortgages easily.

Further, the secondary market assists the flow of capital from cash surplus areas in which available capital exceeds credit demands. Capital deficits occur in those areas where the demand for housing credit exceeds the supply of capital created by the savings of individuals in the area. By balancing capital distribution, geographical differences in interest rates all but disappear, making rates competitive nationally.

The secondary market also allows for portfolio diversification. Loan portfolios are comprised of different types of loans from different geographic locations. Diversification lessens the magnitude of loan losses should an economic hardship or natural disaster occur in a given geographic region and/or with a given loan type.

In short, the secondary market facilitates the buying and selling of mortgages which assures that mortgage money will be available nationwide at competitive rates.

SELLING IN THE SECONDARY MARKET

The primary responsibility of the Marketing Department is to sell loans. The terms of sale are completely negotiable for sales to private investors and more standardized for sales to GSEs and Ginnie Mae. Standardized sales are transacted more quickly and easily than are negotiable sales. However, better pricing and terms can often be obtained from private sources through negotiation.

Loan sale negotiations must address the issues of lender liability (recourse) and servicing responsibility. Many recourse loan sales, for example, require the lender to repurchase any loans that are delinquent or that default within a stated period of time. Nonrecourse sales, on the other hand, usually release the lender from such repurchase liability. Loan sales which establish that the seller will service the loans are called "servicing retained." Sales which stipulate that the seller will not service the loans are called "servicing released." The issues of recourse and servicing affect the price the loan seller receives for the loans.

There are three basic types of loan sales: whole loan, participation loan, and mortgage-backed securities. The sale type is determined by the company, its capital adequacy, loan products, risk tolerance and directives from management. Decisions to sell or not to sell, how to sell, when to sell and what to sell are made based on these constraints.

Whole Loan Sales

A whole loan sale is the sale of 100% of an individual loan or loan package. The loan(s) are generally unsecured and are relatively illiquid. Whole loan sales usually involve large balance or jumbo loans sold to one investor such as a life insurance company or pension fund. The evaluation of whole loans is difficult because each loan is unique and requires extensive documentation.

Participation Loan Sales

A participation loan sale is the sale of a partial interest in a loan or pool of loans, in which the originating lender retains a percentage interest. Mortgage bankers use this type of sale more often for commercial real estate loans than for residential loans. Participation sales have reduced documentation requirements because the originating mortgage banker shares in the default risk.

Mortgage-Backed Security Sales

A mortgage-backed security (MBS) is formed by pooling mortgage loans to form a debt instrument or security collateralized by the loan pool. MBSs provide an investor with an undivided ownership interest in a pool of loans of similar maturity and interest rate. The advantage of selling loans as securities includes standardized commitments to investors, reduced documentation and, most important, liquidity.

The greatest volume of MBSs are issued by Fannie Mae, Freddie Mac and Ginnie Mae. These MBSs are popular among lenders because standardization has made loan sales efficient and easy. Investors also favor these MBS programs because repayment of the securities is backed by the full faith and credit of the U.S. Government (for Ginnie Mae) and by GSE status (for Fannie Mae and Freddie Mac).

Private institutions also issue MBSs on a more limited scale. These securities are sold through investment bankers. Although repayment of the security is not guaranteed in the same manner as with GSE securities, other credit enhancements such as mortgage insurance and pool insurance make them attractive.

Managing the Pipeline

Loans in the pipeline and potentially available for sale are tracked by some sort of pipeline report. The report is usually generated from an automated system and indicates the amount and timing of loans for closing. Based on experience and market conditions, Marketing uses the report to estimate the percentage of loans that will close and arranges coverage for those loans. Coverage assigns investor commitments or other risk management strategies to the pipeline to manage the risk of interest rate changes. A change in interest rate affects the price at which loans are sold.

Investor Commitments

Loan sales are confirmed by investor commitments. The investor commitment is a document evidencing the obligation of the mortgage banker to sell and the obligation of the investor to buy a loan or loan pool.

Investor commitments detail the terms, requirements, and delivery dates required to complete loan sales. A typical commitment may include specifications for the price, type and volume of loans, interest rates, loan age, geographic locations and loan file documentation. This document dictates production schedules and future servicing portfolio additions.

The two main categories of investor commitments are mandatory and optional. The mandatory commitment requires performance, meaning the mortgage banker must sell the loans and the investor must buy the loans according to the terms of the commitment. It carries considerable risk, should the loans be unavailable for delivery or should market interest rates fall. However, these risks are offset by a higher loan price. The optional commitment has an "out" for the mortgage banker, for which the mortgage banker pays a fee. The option not to deliver loans can be chosen, which gives the mortgage banker the opportunity to obtain a better loan price in the market, if it is available.

Pricing

To the Marketing Department, price is the amount the investor pays to purchase loans. To the Production Department, price is the interest rate and discount that can be offered borrowers. Marketing must balance the mandates of production for unique mortgage programs with competitive pricing with orders from senior management to achieve the firm's profit goal. In most cases, the objective is to do no worse than break even. Nonetheless, in certain rate environments, many lenders prefer to subsidize prices over set periods of time in order to protect market share. Regardless of strategy, however, losses will occur if pricing to borrowers is not in sync with pricing from investors.

RISK MANAGEMENT

Marketing strives to achieve volume and preserve value of the mortgage pipeline for sale in the secondary mortgage market. Numerous risks are inherent in marketing that can undermine this objective. These risks relate to interest rate volatility, product selection, pipeline fallout and investor credit.

Interest rate risk results from volatile interest rates. A change in interest rates that occurs between loan origination and loan sale can leave the lender with unsalable loans or loans which must be sold at a discount because rates have risen. Loans with higher interest rates have higher yields and are more attractive to investors.

Hedging is one way to manage interest rate risk. Hedging is risk transfer through the use of hedge instruments. Some of these instruments include investor commitments, futures and options. The simplest way to hedge interest rate risk is to lock in loan prices at the time of origination for sale and delivery in the future.

Product risk occurs when no market exists for a particular loan product by the time that product is available to be sold. Loan types often experience peaks and valleys in popularity, depending on prevailing economic conditions. As borrowers or investors lose interest in a particular loan type, loan inventory may become unsalable. By coordinating investor requirements with borrower needs, product risk can be minimized.

Pipeline fallout results from loans in the pipeline that fail to close. This may occur because the property sale falls through or the borrower finds a better interest rate with another lender. In either case, a lender must apply coverage prudently to the mortgage pipeline to compensate for some degree of fallout. Most lenders will assume a certain percentage of future fallout when making hedging decisions — generally reflecting current fallout rates.

Investor credit risk results when an investor refuses delivery or cannot take delivery of loans because of its own financial difficulties. An investigation of the investor's reputation is the best way to avoid credit risk. Financial statements and reference should be obtained prior to entering into a commitment.

LOAN ORIGINATION 3

Loan origination is the process by which mortgage bankers create residential mortgages. It involves external relationships between borrowers and loan officers and internal relationships between loan officers and the departments of processing, underwriting and loan closing.

Loan origination functions include:

- developing customers,

- recommending loan programs,

- taking loan applications,

- requesting loan documentation and verifications and

- making regulatory disclosures.

GENERATING MORTGAGE BANKING BUSINESS

The loan originator or loan officer plays a key role in loan origination. The loan officer is responsible for seeking out loan applicants. Most of the loan officer's business comes from real estate agents and brokers, builders and developers, consumer direct (walk-ins) and affinity sources.

The origination of resale loans is normally the result of lender referrals from real estate agents and brokers. Potential homebuyers using the services of real estate agents or brokers in transacting real estate purchases traditionally depend on these agents to recommend lenders. The recommendation of a specific lender is based on the loan officer's reputation for originating loans in a timely manner and on the lender's reputation for offering competitive loan programs and interest rates.

Builder and developer originations involve making new construction and construction-to-permanent loans. To develop builder business, loan officers often seek out new financing commitments with builders. Once such a relationship is established, builders and developers tend to remain loyal to particular lenders that consistently provide superior service.

Direct originations account for only a small percentage of a lender's business in typical markets. In low interest rate refinance markets, however, walk-ins can be a significant source of good business. Walk-in loans typically occur in response to lender advertising or word-of-mouth recommendations from prior customers. Consumer-direct business is also obtained through consumer advertising, mailings, home computer access and, indirectly, via Computerized Loan Origination (CLO) networks.

Affinity originations traditionally account for a very small portion of most residential mortgage business. However, the percentage has grown in recent years as more borrowers are influenced through nontraditional referral networks — particularly ones which can offer additional services or assistance. Some examples of affinity sources include employer referrals and relocations, insurance agents, investment brokers, financial planners, shopping malls, rental agents, and banks, thrifts and credit unions which do not have mortgage departments.

QUALITIES AND RESPONSIBILITIES OF THE LOAN ORIGINATOR

Loan officers must have excellent sales skills to sell themselves, their companies and their products. Since the loan officer is usually the only person a borrower meets face-to-face at a particular mortgage company, this person must possess a high degree of personal integrity. Of equal importance are well-developed presentation skills and a thorough knowledge of mortgage lending practices and products, origination market area and competitive forces.

The loan originator is responsible for the initial interview with the prospective borrower. During the interview, the originator reviews the sales contract for the subject property and pre-qualifies the applicant to determine if the applicant can afford the property. Pre-qualification includes the determination of two basic ratios:

- housing-to-income ratio and

- total debt-to-income ratio.

The housing-to-income ratio divides the total monthly housing expense (principal, interest, escrows, mortgage insurance premium and homeowner's fees) by the applicant's monthly gross income (income before any deductions). An acceptable ratio should generally not exceed 28% for conventional loans and 29% for government loans. Private investors and state government agencies may have other percentage requirements.

The total debt-to-income ratio divides total monthly debts (prospective housing expense plus other consumer debts such as car loans, student loans and credit cards) by the applicant's gross monthly income. An acceptable ratio should generally not exceed 36% for conventional loans and 41% for government loans. Again, these requirements vary among private investors and others.

If the pre-qualification ratios are unacceptably high, the loan officer should suggest practical alternatives to the applicant. One alternative may be to establish the maximum monthly mortgage payment the applicant can afford given their present financial position. Another is to suggest ways the applicant can improve their financial position.

In many circumstances, the loan officer also obtains a preliminary credit report at the pre-qualification stage. These credit reports — known as "in file" reports — are typically obtained directly from one or more credit repositories and may therefore include inaccurate information. They can, however, enable the loan officer to immediately verify monthly debt payment information supplied by the applicant as well as preview the applicant's credit history. Any potential problem areas — such as past late payments or accounts not belonging to the applicant — can then begin to be addressed at this stage.

MORTGAGE BANKING LOAN PROGRAMS

If the applicant comes to the loan officer with a property already selected and a sales contract in hand, the contract may specify the type of financing to be used, (ARM, Fixed or Buydown), as well

as the type of program (FHA, VA, FmHA or conventional.) If it does not, the loan officer must review available loan programs with the applicant, so that an appropriate selection is made.

Mortgage companies look for products and programs that are competitive in their originating markets, profitable to sell in the secondary market and compatible with their servicing capabilities. Borrowers look for products and programs they can understand and that are compatible with their current and potential earnings. Some of the more popular financing options are as follows:

Fixed-rate mortgages (FRMs) allow borrowers to fully amortize a mortgage by making equal monthly payments of principal and interest to the lender for a pre-determined term, usually 15 or 30 years. The interest rate never changes and borrowers can budget for the payments with certainty.

Adjustable-rate mortgages (ARMs) or variable-rate mortgages have an interest rate that increases or decreases over the life of the loan based on market conditions. The start rate is normally lower than the rate offered on a fixed-rate mortgage. Changes in the interest rate are determined by a financial index. The most common indices are the one-year, three-year and five-year Treasury bills (T-bills), the California 11th District Cost of Funds Index (COFI) and the Prime Rate posted by the Federal Reserve.

Although ARMs have low initial interest rates, payment patterns are uncertain.

Balloon mortgages generally consist of equal monthly payments based on a 15- to 30-year amortization, but do not fully amortize the loan. At the end of the balloon term, generally 3, 5, 7 or 10 years, a large final payment is due, equal to the remaining balance on the loan. Balloon rates are usually lower than FRMs. They are a beneficial financing option for borrowers intending to sell their homes and pay off their mortgages prior to the balloon due date.

Graduated payment mortgages (GPMs) are for homebuyers who expect to be able to make larger monthly payments as their income grows. GPMs are similar to fixed-rate mortgages in that monthly payments are amortized over 15 or 30 years. However, payments during the early years of the GPM are lower than what would be required on a similar fixed-rate mortgage and are insufficient to fully amortize the loan. This interest deficit is added to the outstanding loan balance to offset the lower payments and negative amortization results. At a set point in time (approximately 5-10 years out), the GPM payment exceeds the FRM payment and the balance begins to be paid off.

Growing equity mortgages (GEMs) are similar to GPMs in structure, but are used by borrowers for a completely different purpose. The GEM uses a fixed-rate mortgage with payments that rise yearly until the mortgage is paid off. Unlike the GPM, the lender applies the payment hike directly to the outstanding balance, creating a faster payoff of the mortgage debt. Although the mortgage loan is scheduled to end in 30 years, the loan is often paid off in less than 15 years.

Bi-weekly mortgages are similar to standard FRMs or ARMs. The difference is in the number of payments made each year. Normally, the borrower makes monthly payments, or 12 payments a year. With a bi-weekly mortgage, payments are made every two weeks, totaling 26 (or possibly 27) half-payments each year. Two advantages of this option are that payments can more easily be made directly from a bank account, and the loan is actually paid off more quickly.

Reverse mortgages are intended for individuals who already own a home with no or very little indebtedness. These individuals, usually elderly, desire to remain in their homes, need cash to meet expenses, but do not wish to make repayment while they are still living in the home. With a reverse mortgage, the lender makes either a one-time or periodic payments to the borrower. The principal andinterest paid accumulates against the property, resulting in negative amortization. Repayment of the resultant balance is generally only required upon the borrower's death or sale of the property, depending on the loan's specific terms.

These are only a few of the loan programs available. New products and remakes/combinations of old products frequently appear and disappear in a lender's line of loan programs. The popularity of particular loan programs varies with the geographic region and economic cycles. A loan originator must know the loan programs their mortgage lending firm offers and be able to recommend programs that meet each applicant's needs.

Once the borrower chooses a loan program, the interest rate and any discount points can be "locked in" or guaranteed for a period of time — generally 30 or 60 days. For new construction, the lock-in period is often much longer. Once locked in, the loan must generally be closed prior to the lock-in expiration date in order to preserve the rate guarantee.

COMPLETION OF THE LOAN APPLICATION

The loan application is usually the first document in the borrower's loan file. It must be complete, accurate and legible. The Uniform Residential Loan Application (URLA) form is acceptable to virtually all lenders and investors. This application requests information about the borrower and the subject property. Information can be written onto the application or entered via a laptop or other computer terminal. The information requested includes:

- mortgage information (loan program, amount, rate, term),

- applicant's address, phone number and social security number (must include at least the last two years of address information),

- applicant's income (primary, rental, interest and other),

- applicant's employer, address and phone number (must include at least the last two years of employment information),

- applicant's assets (cash, stocks, real estate and businesses),

- applicant's liabilities (credit cards, consumer and real estate loans),

- property address and sales price and

- legal information (how title will be held, past judgments, certifications, etc.).

In addition to completing the loan application, supporting documentation is requested from the applicant. The precise documentation requirements will vary depending on the type of loan, type of income, type of debts, etc. Such documentation includes:

- Certificate of Eligibility (COE), if applying for a VA loan,

- past W-2s, current pay stubs, evidence of other income,

- past tax returns,

- financial statements (profit & loss, etc.),

- bank statements (savings, checking, investments),

- debt statements (account numbers, addresses, etc.) and

- property sales contract.

Documentation supplied by the applicant is added to the loan file. This file is an important part of the loan process, since it is passed through every mortgage banking department and parts are eventually forwarded to the investor who purchases the loan.

The processor is responsible for confirming the applicant's information by obtaining verifications of bank deposits, investments and employment. If required by the loan program, the processor orders a credit report which details the borrower's credit history. The processor also orders an appraisal which verifies the value of the subject property.

Origination fees are normally charged to the applicant to cover the cost of processing the loan. In addition, discount points are charged in accordance with the "lock-in" rate agreed upon with the loan officer. These discount points enable the lender to offer interest rates that are lower than those requested by secondary mortgage market investors. Some applicants prefer to pay higher interest rates than those the investors seek. In these cases, the "premium rate"

enables the lender to pay all or a portion of the applicant's closing costs.

Origination fees can be financed on some types of loans, but discount points can only rarely be financed. Property sellers often pay points and other fees at closing, if agreed upon in the sales contract. The amounts of such payments, called concessions, are limited by agencies and investors in order to protect the integrity of the property's appraised value.

REGULATORY COMPLIANCE

The mortgage banking process is highly regulated. Appropriate regulatory disclosure is particularly vital during the application stage. Federal and state laws have been implemented to protect and inform the applicant at this stage. The three most basic federal rules are:

- Equal Credit Opportunity Act (ECOA)

- Real Estate Settlement Procedures Act (RESPA)

- Truth-in-Lending Act (TiL)

ECOA prohibits discrimination based on an applicant's race, sex, marital status, national origin, age, religion, color, income derived from public assistance or the applicant's exercise of their rights under the Consumer Credit Protection Act. ECOA requires the lender to notify the applicant of their loan status within 30 days of application. It also requires lenders to collect the race and sex of each applicant for government monitoring purposes.

RESPA prohibits kickbacks and referral fees amongst lenders, real estate professionals, builders and other settlement service providers. RESPA also requires lenders to provide applicants, within three days of application, a Good Faith Estimate (GFE) disclosure of all settlement costs the applicant is expected to incur accompanied by an information booklet that describes the loan closing process. A final itemization of all charges (HUD-1 Settlement Statement) is required at closing. RESPA also regulates the amounts of fees lenders are able to collect for the purpose of establishing and administering escrow accounts to pay real estate taxes, hazard insurance and other housing expenses.

Truth-in-Lending requires lenders to disclose to applicants within three days of application all direct and indirect costs related to the prospective financing, including interest, mortgage insurance, points and loan fees. This disclosure must include a standard annual percentage rate (APR) that theoretically enables consumers to compare varying loan products/terms from one lender to another. Applicants for ARMs must receive additional disclosure statement(s) at application setting out sample terms for every ARM program in which they are interested. Truth-in-Lending requires the use of the APR in all consumer advertisements which reference credit terms (payment or interest rate.)

APPLICATION FOLLOW-UP

The loan officer's duties continue after loan application, document collection and regulatory disclosure. The loan officer is responsible for following the loan from origination through funding. The loan officer communicates with the applicant on their loan approval status and the anticipated closing date. The loan officer also communicates with internal departments — processing, underwriting and closing — to ensure the loan progresses according to schedule.

Loan officers are normally compensated by commission payable after closing. They are also dependent on an excellent service record to ensure that their referral sources remain satisfied. They therefore have a significant vested interest in getting every loan closed and funded smoothly.

LOAN PROCESSING 4

Loan processing is the gathering of loan documents and verifications to complete the loan file. Accuracy and completeness are critical to processing to ensure that delays do not lengthen the review period. The condition of the loan file is paramount to the underwriting decision to fund or reject the loan.

Loan processing functions include:

- assembling loan files,

- ordering and assembling verifications, appraisals, credit reports and other necessary documents,

- reviewing all documents for signatures, completeness, accuracy and legibility, and

- analyzing the final package to ensure investor requirements are met.

LOAN FILE SETUP

The processor initially inventories new loan files to see what documents are missing, and reviews documents in the file for completeness and signatures, where necessary. The processor requests of the applicant missing documents, mails verification forms and orders the credit report and property appraisal. By maintaining a log (either on paper or in an automated production system) of document requests and mailings by date, the processor can easily report on the status of each loan in progress.

Verification forms are sent directly to depositories and employers, and should not pass through the hands of the applicant, the seller, the loan originator or the real estate agent. Hand-delivery via one of these individuals is an open invitation to fraud.

Upon receipt of requested loan documents, the processor logs in and checks the documents for potential errors, omissions and discrepancies from the loan application. If the processor discovers any inconsistencies, they are resolved. In most lender shops, the processor's primary objective is to gather accurate facts — not to draw conclusions. However, for some lenders, the processor — particularly if very experienced — is a key decision-maker on whether a loan is submitted to Underwriting for review, or is rejected prior to submission.

The basic documents comprising the loan file are described below. Mortgage banking firms and investors may have specific underwriting standards or investment criteria that require additional documentation.

- Loan application — handwritten, typed or computer-generated.

- Real estate sales contract — a copy of the sales contract signed by the buyers and sellers of the real estate securing the prospective mortgage. The sales contract discloses to the lender the location of the property, the purchase price, contingencies and special considerations that may affect the condition of the property.

- Verification of Employment (VOE) — forms signed by the applicant(s) and sent to the applicant's employer. Copies of the applicant's pay stubs, W-2s and bank statements may be included. The VOE establishes stable employment and income sufficient to meet loan payments. Self-employment is verified by personal financial statements and a corporate profit and loss statement.

- Verification of Deposit (VOD) — forms signed by the applicant(s) and sent to the applicant's banking institution(s) and investment broker(s) to confirm bank deposits, stocks, bonds and other investments. The VOD establishes that sufficient cash to meet closing requirements is available.

- Credit report — A report issued by a consumer credit reporting agency that discloses the applicant's credit accounts and payment history, outstanding debts, and liens and judgments of public record. Whereas an "in-file" report provides just basic credit information, mortgage bankers often require a full or "Residential Mortgage Credit Report" (RMCR) that meets specific GSE and federal agency criteria. An RMCR confirms employment as well as credit information.

- Appraisal — A report made by a professional appraiser which establishes the current market value of the property securing the prospective mortgage. Federal agencies and GSEs require the use of a state-licensed or certified appraiser. The appraisal justifies the loan amount being requested.

- Regulatory disclosure statements — copies of disclosure statements that show compliance with applicable laws — as evidenced by each applicant's signature.

PROCESSING DIFFERENT LOAN TYPES

The four basic types of loans the loan processor encounters are FHA, VA, FmHA and conventional. While the principles of processing are the same regardless of loan type, there are some technical differences in the way the loan processor handles each type of loan.

FHA Loans

FHA processing is a two-step process of appraisal acceptance and FHA loan commitment.

The mortgage banker can approve and close an FHA loan if the firm holds Direct Endorsement (DE) authority. Otherwise, the loan must be presented to the appropriate FHA office for review and approval prior to closing.

The appraisal, performed by a staff or a fee appraiser, must meet specific FHA review standards. If the property is acceptable, the mortgage banker's DE Underwriter issues a Conditional Commitment which establishes the market value of the property for mortgage insurance purposes.

VA Loans

VA processing is also a two-step process of appraisal acceptance and VA loan guarantee. Since the VA guarantees up to a specified percentage of the loan for eligible veterans, an initial step in VA processing is to establish the veteran's basic eligibility and the amount of guarantee to which the veteran is entitled.

The mortgage banker can approve and close a VA loan if the firm has VA Automatic authority. Otherwise, the loan must be presented to the VA for review and approval prior to closing.

The appraisal, performed by a VA-selected fee appraiser, must meet specific VA review standards. If the property is acceptable, the VA issues a Certificate of Reasonable Value (CRV) which establishes the current market value of the property. If the lender is approved for the Lender Appraisal Processing Program (LAPP), the CRV is sent directly by the appraiser to the lender's VA Appraisal Reviewer. If the lender is not approved for LAPP, the CRV must first be reviewed by the VA.

The final loan file is submitted to the mortgage banker's VA Automatic Underwriter or directly to the VA. If the veteran is deemed eligible, the loan is closed and submitted to the VA as approved. The VA then reviews the file to ensure that all lender compliance requirements are met. If they are, the VA guarantees the loan.

FmHA Loans

Rural housing loans guaranteed by FmHA are processed differently from FHA and VA loans. FmHA loans must be approved by the appropriate local office prior to funding. The FmHA review confirms that the property is located in a rural area, that the applicant's total family income does not exceed the relevant county limitation and that the applicant would not qualify for conventional financing. The review also confirms that sufficient FmHA funding exists to cover the loan.

Once approved by FmHA, the lender may close and fund the loan. FmHA issues a guarantee and the lender may then deliver the loan to the secondary market.

Conventional Loans

Conventional processing requires no government agency reviews or approvals. Full responsibility for the acceptability of the property and the applicant rests with the mortgage banker. Normally, the downpayment required is greater than for FHA, VA or FmHA loans to reduce the mortgage banker's risk. Loan amounts that exceed 80% of the value of the property (LTV ratio) in all but the rarest circumstances require private mortgage insurance (MI). MI companies, however, generally prefer not to insure loans with LTVs over 95% — due to the relatively high risk and to legal restrictions in many states.

Investors that buy conventional loans have a variety of requirements. The handling and processing of conventional loans differs depending on the purchasing investor. The processor is responsible for turning over to underwriting complete loan files, based on the requirements of the purchasing investor.

UNDERWRITING 5

Underwriting is the evaluation of documents comprising the loan file to determine if the loan should be approved or denied. In essence, underwriting analyzes the lender's risk in making a loan. Strict underwriting guidelines lessen risk and result in high quality loans. Lax underwriting procedures produce loans which default and are not salable in the secondary mortgage market.

Loan underwriting functions include:

- re-verifying loan files for completeness, accuracy and legibility,

- verifying that all loan files meet underwriting guidelines and investor requirements,

- calculating qualifying ratios,

- reviewing appraisals,

- reviewing and evaluating loan file documentation and

- approving or denying loans.

QUALITIES AND RESPONSIBILITIES OF THE UNDERWRITER

The underwriter has the ultimate responsibility to approve or deny loans based on underwriting guidelines established by the lending firm, specific requirements of the investor purchasing the loan and the contents of the loan file.

A good underwriter is objective in decision making, yet understands that there is flexibility in underwriting guidelines. Each loan file is unique, with strengths and weaknesses that in some cases offset each other.

Underwriting guidelines are largely nonstandardized. FHA, VA, FmHA and conventional loan guidelines differ, as do the loan requirements of different investors. It is important for underwriters to know the various guidelines and when to follow them.

The reputation of a mortgage banking company and its underwriting staff is related to the quality of mortgages it sells to investors. Investor relationships based on mutual trust and respect are essential to success in the mortgage banking business. Loan defaults taint this relationship.

FOUR "Cs" OF UNDERWRITING

The underwriting review examines the borrower, in terms of creditworthiness and willingness to repay the mortgage according to its terms, and the property, as security sufficient in value and physical condition to recover the outstanding loan amount in the case of default. "The Four Cs of Underwriting" refer to the underwriting review of:

- collateral,

- capacity,

- character and

- capital.

Collateral refers to the underwriter's evaluation of the subject property using a professionally prepared appraisal. The appraisal contains two important pieces of data, namely an estimate of the property's value and comments on the property's physical condition.

The basis for the lender to establish the maximum loan amount the property can secure is the lower of the property's appraised value or the sales price stated in the sales contract. For conventional loans, the lender is normally willing to lend 80% of the property's value (80% LTV). For FHA loans, the maximum LTV is 98.75% for loans at or below $50,000 and 97.75% otherwise. For VA and FmHA loans, the LTV may exceed 100% in certain instances, since no downpayment is required.

The concern for the lender in establishing an acceptable LTV is the ability to recoup the outstanding mortgage amount should the loan default. Higher LTVs are allowed for FHA, VA and FmHA loans because of the government insurance and guarantees that back them. Higher LTVs are also allowed on some special programs designed to assist underserved markets, but these programs are subsidized and limited by the GSEs and HFAs that administer them.

The condition of the property is important to the underwriter in assessing sufficient collateral value to support the loan. A poorly maintained property brings a lower price at foreclosure sale and also gives the borrower less incentive to cure payment delinquencies. Appraisers traditionally comment on the con-dition of the appraised property on the appraisal form. These remarks do not preclude loans from being made on "fixer-upper" properties. However, they do alert the underwriter to ensure that the borrower's financial resources are sufficient to make the necessary improvements.

Capacity refers to the applicant's ability to make monthly housing payments, i.e. the applicant's financial resources. Acceptable sources of income may include:

- salary of the applicant and co-applicant, if any,

- overtime pay,

- part-time and second job income,

- bonuses and commissions, interest and dividends,
- investments (such as real estate),

- self-employment, partner-ships, corporations,

- welfare or Social Security receipts and

- alimony or child support.

The applicant's income is typically derived from salary, overtime pay and part-time or second job income. W-2s and VOEs support the amount from which the underwriter calculates the monthly income. If the applicant is self-employed, two years' tax returns are required. Self-employment income is generally based on the average of the past two years' earnings. Income from alimony or child support requires a letter from the payee stating the amount being paid and the duration of the payments.

Qualifying ratios are calculated using the monthly income figure. The ratios, housing-to-income and total debt-to-income, are the same ratios calculated at pre-qualification, except now they are supported by verified loan file data. The ratios must meet different investor requirements for acceptable amounts, and calculation methods which differ for FHA, VA, FmHA and conventional loans. Compensating factors, such as a large downpayment, substantial capital investments, or the potential for increased earnings, can override ratios that fail to meet underwriting requirements. The underwriter is responsible for documenting specific compensating factors that override nonconforming ratios.

Character refers to the applicant's motivation to make monthly mortgage payments. The credit report summarizes the applicant's motivation by providing a history of credit payment performance. It reveals slow or delinquent payments, foreclosures and bankruptcies.

The underwriter investigates occurrences of bad credit to determine if they represent an ongoing problem or are simply isolated cases beyond the applicant's control. Written explanations are requested from the applicant which become part of the loan file. A history of bad credit is not a basis for automatic denial, especially if evidence is present that the borrower has corrected past problems. Bad credit is, however, a signal to the underwriter of increased risk. In all cases, existing credit problems must be cured before loan closing.

Capital refers to the liquid assets the borrower has available to make the downpayment on the loan, meet loan closing costs and have on hand reserves necessary to make the initial mortgage payments. It is possible that the prospective borrower is able to make the monthly mortgage payments, but lacks the cash to close. Or, the borrower may be able to close, but will be financially depleted by doing so. Capital assets which the underwriter looks toward for down payment and closing costs include:

- checking and savings accounts,

- stocks, bonds and investments,

- insurance policies,

- gifts or inheritances,

- IRA/Keough accounts or

- sale proceeds from an existing home.

The underwriter evaluates the capital requirements against the borrower's capital resources and documents it in the loan file. A gift letter must be obtained to verify a sizable gift and to ensure that the intent of the giver is not to be repaid. For property sale proceeds, a copy of the sales contract is required. IRA/Keough accounts should be verified as to withdrawal privileges and withdrawal penalties, if any.

THE UNDERWRITING DECISION

Underwriting is often more art than science. It requires studied and experienced judgment.

Evaluations of collateral, capacity, character and capital must be supported by confirmed data which the underwriter interprets within the context of each applicant and subject property. At times, circumstances influencing the underwriting decision are so complex that the final decision is made by committee.

Time is of the essence in rendering the underwriting decision. Since most loan applications carry a 30-, 45- or 60-day lock-in period, loan closing must occur within that period to obtain the interest rate and loan terms stated at origination. Inability to approve and close the loan within the lock-in period tarnishes the lender's reputation.

As a final step, the underwriter executes an underwriting decision. The loan officer communicates the decision to the loan applicant and, if an approval, confirms the decision with a written loan commitment. The complete loan file is then sent to the closing department.

If the loan is rejected, a denial letter must be sent to the applicant(s) stating the reason(s) for the denial and including the name and address of the source of any third-party information that contributed to the denial decision (normally the credit bureau and/or appraiser.) This procedure must be followed whether a denial decision is made by an underwriter, loan officer or other lender employee.

LOAN CLOSING

6

Loan closing is the legal execution of the loan. This includes the signing and recordation of all loan documents creating the mortgage and the disbursement of loan funds. At loan closing, the title to the property passes from the seller to the buyer. Simultaneously, the buyer receives the mortgage funds to purchase the property, while pledging the property as security for repayment of the debt.

Closing is of particular importance to the mortgage banker because it establishes a first lien on the property and creates an enforceable debt. In other words, it gives the mortgage banker the right to expect repayment of the borrowed funds and recourse should the borrower default on the loan.

Every step preceding the closing process and those involved in the loan closing process must be performed meticulously. If closing fails to take place, the loan origination, processing and underwriting functions have been done in vain and

the expense of performing those functions is unrecoverable. Also, loans committed for sale are unavailable to meet delivery dates and anticipated servicing income is lost because no new loans are produced to add to the servicing portfolio.

Loan closing functions include:

- preparing and assembling closing documents,

- funding mortgage loans and

- recording signed closing documents.

PREPARING AND ASSEMBLING CLOSING DOCUMENTS

The required closing documents vary based on requirements imposed by the state, the mortgage company, the loan program and the loan type. It is important for loan closing personnel to keep abreast of changing laws and regulations within each of the markets the mortgage banker serves.

Seven documents form the basis for the closing package. These documents include the mortgage instrument, the note, the deed, the HUD-1 Settlement Statement, the final TiL disclosure, the title insurance policy and the hazard insurance policy.

The *mortgage instrument* evidences the mortgage lender's security interest in the real property. In most states this instrument is a "mortgage," while in others it is a "deed of trust," or a "security trust deed." The mortgage instrument gives a complete legal description of the property and provides for conveyance of the property from the borrower (mortgagor) to the lender (mortgagee) in the case of default on the note.

The traditional mortgage involves only two parties, the lender and the borrower. The deed of trust or security trust deed, on the other hand, is a multiparty instrument which, in case of default, conveys title to the real property to a trustee until such time as the debt is satisfied. Absent a default, title to the real property is generally held by the borrower, but can be held by either borrower or lender, depending on state law.

The *mortgage note* is a promissory note that creates a legal obligation of the borrower to repay the debt secured by the mortgage. The note states the date of loan closing; the loan amount and interest rate; when, where, and how often payments are to be made; and the date by which the borrower must pay the loan in full. If an assumption clause is included, the obligation for the debt can be transferred to another party upon sale of the property.

The note is negotiable. This allows the mortgage lender to assign the loan upon sale into the secondary mortgage market. Once the debt is repaid in full, a notice of satisfaction is recorded. This clears the lien on the property's title.

The *deed* conveys title to the property from the seller to the buyer. The statute of frauds requires that the deed be in writing and signed by the grantor.

The *HUD-1 Settlement Statement* is required by RESPA. The HUD-1 provides the buyer and seller of the property with full disclosure of closing costs. It establishes the actual dollar amount of funds that the borrower must bring to the closing table and itemizes how and to whom buyer, seller and lender funds are to be disbursed.

The final *Truth-in-Lending* disclosure reveals the final APR and other relevant financing terms. It is only necessary if the initial TiL disclosure is marked "estimate" or the terms or APR have changed sufficiently since loan application.

The *title insurance policy* or *binder* evidences that an examination of public title records has been made to disclose all facts regarding ownership of the subject property, encumbrances, tax liens or other interests. The title examination establishes who can execute the mortgage to encumber the property. The title policy is insurance for the lender that no liens or interests other than those disclosed on the policy will precede the security interest established by the mortgage.

The *hazard insurance policy* or binder evidences insurance taken out on the subject property against losses caused by fire, wind or other natural disasters. The policy is required by lenders as well as investors to protect their security interests in case of disaster. In addition to the hazard policy, if the property is located in a designated flood area, a separate flood insurance policy is required.

Depending on lender or investor specifications or the loan type, there may be additional closing documents. Some of these may include:

- adjustable rate rider — acknowledges an ARM with a variable interest rate,

- assignment of mortgage — assigns the mortgage to a permanent investor,

- building restrictions and certificates of occupancy — for new construction,

- real estate sales contract — verifies the property sale,

- disbursement papers — gives guidelines to disburse mortgage funds,

- escrow agreement — specifies duty to pay taxes and insurance,

- homeowners association agreement — explains subdivision restrictions,

- private mortgage insurance commitment — verifies private insurance,

- FHA or VA commitments and disclosures — verifies DE/ Automatic approval and applicant compliance,

- survey — confirms property size, location and any encroachments, hold harmless letters and

- termite certificate — states the presence or absence of termites.

It is the responsibility of the loan closer to ensure that each closing document is accurate and precise. Loan terms and dates contained in the mortgage note must agree with every other document. The borrower's name must be written consistently. The loan closer must be a detail-oriented person whose main objective is to ensure that closing results in a marketable loan.

FUNDING THE MORTGAGE LOAN

Depending on local custom and the mortgage banker's requirements, loan closing can be handled by an attorney outside the firm, a title insurance company, an escrow agent, or closing staff of the mortgage banker. If closing is performed outside the firm, an insured closing letter is obtained to protect the mortgage firm against embezzlement of funds or failure to follow closing instructions.

The closing agent explains the closing documents to the closing parties and obtains the buyer's and seller's signatures on the required documents. Each signature must be signed identically to the typed name on each document. The funds, usually obtained from the mortgage banker's short-term line of credit at a warehouse bank, are then disbursed by check. At this point, physical closing is complete.

RECORDING THE MORTGAGE DOCUMENTS

The signed mortgage documents are recorded at the local courthouse to make public record of the security interest (in the form of a mortgage or deed of trust) and assignment of the mortgage, if any. Recording protects the borrower and the mortgage banker from competing claims against the property and creates a first lien on the property. Should the borrower default on the loan, the court pays foreclosure claims in the order in which they were recorded (with the exception of tax liens, which supersede all liens.) Therefore, although recording can take a year or longer in some jurisdictions, it is important to record the deed as soon as possible following loan closing.

MORTGAGE WAREHOUSING ▐ 7

Mortgage warehousing is the financing of loans from closing until sale to an investor. The money to finance the loans is in most cases borrowed through a short-term, revolving line of credit established with one or more commercial banks. An alternative to borrowing is using repurchase lines or commercial paper.

Since mortgage bankers are not highly capitalized, they depend on warehouse lines of credit to fund their operations. Warehousing permits increased loan originations, which translates to an increased return on investment. The use of borrowed funds to increase return on investment is called leverage.

Warehousing functions include:

- negotiating lines of credit,

- monitoring interest rates and fees on lines of credit,

- maintaining adequate compensating balances,

- maintaining required warehouse documentation,

- coordinating investor commitments with the warehouse bank and

- facilitating disbursements to fund loans.

WAREHOUSE LINES OF CREDIT

Mortgage bankers using warehouse lines of credit to fund their operations typically obtain one or more lines. Each line is approved to a specified dollar amount limited by the mortgage banker's capital as disclosed on financial statements of the firm. The capital collateralizes the line. If one line is insufficient to fund all of a mortgage banker's production, additional lines or alternative sources of funds must be obtained.

The line amount on loan to the mortgage banker at any point in time is called "outstandings." Outstandings are short-term because the funds are only needed until the loans are delivered to the investor that previously committed to purchase them. Outstandings are also "revolving" because the funds are borrowed and repaid repeatedly as new loans are closed, funded and sold to investors.

INTEREST RATES, FEES AND COMPENSATING BALANCES

The interest rate charged on outstandings is normally floating and is tied to the warehouse bank's prime rate. This rate, whether fixed or floating, is negotiated between the bank(s) and the mortgage banker. Rates generally vary from prime rate to 1% or 2% above the prime rate. In addition to interest, most warehouse banks require additional compensation for making credit available. Such compensation takes the form of fees or compensating balances.

The most common fee is the warehouse commitment fee, an annual charge calculated as a percentage of the approved line amount. Another common fee is the non-use fee. This fee is calculated as a percentage of the average unused line balance.

Compensating balances are escrows kept in demand deposit accounts at the warehouse bank. The escrows represent moneys collected by the mortgage banker from borrowers for the payment of hazard insurance, property taxes and (in some cases) mortgage insurance premiums. Compensating balances can be required as a stated percentage of the approved line or a percentage of the average

outstandings or a combination of both. They benefit the warehouse bank by collateralizing the line and increasing the warehouse bank's deposit base. Compensating balances that exceed the required amount are often used to buy down the interest rate on the warehouse line.

WAREHOUSE SPREAD

Warehouse spread is the difference between the interest rate on the warehouse line and the interest rate being paid on mortgages funded by the line. It is one of several sources of income for the mortgage banker. This income can be enhanced by responsible management of the warehouse line, i.e. limiting the duration of outstandings and maintaining high compensating balances.

COLLATERAL

A warehouse line of credit is secured, i.e. it is collateralized by assignments of mortgage notes to the warehouse bank. The warehouse bank requests the mortgage notes to be committed for purchase by an investor at the time they are warehoused. This preserves the values of the warehouse bank's collateral should there be an upward movement in interest rates. For further protection, most warehouse banks require that they approve the investors to whom their mortgage banking customers are selling loans, since these investors are the warehouse bank's source of repayment. For financially sound, well-capitalized mortgage banking customers, the warehouse bank may allow a portion of the line to be made available to fund uncommitted loans.

For committed loans, the warehouse bank allows the mortgage banker to borrow near the market value of the loans or 99 percent. For uncommitted loans, a lesser amount is advanced based on current market yields. The difference between the line advance allowed by the warehouse bank and the amount needed to fund loan closings 100% is called a haircut.

REQUIRED DOCUMENTATION

The warehouse bank requires documentation on each loan being funded. The most important document is the original, signed mortgage note endorsed in blank. This document evidences the debt due from the borrower.

The mortgage note is sold to the investor. The endorsement is in blank in case for any reason the mortgage banker cannot honor its obligation to repay the credit line. In this situation, the warehouse bank takes ownership of the note by endorsing it to itself and delivers it into the existing investor commitment, if possible, or sells it to another investor to obtain repayment. The request for advances, mortgage, mortgage assignment, title insurance binder and investor commitment are also important documents to the warehouse bank from a collateral standpoint. These documents reconstruct the loan file in the event the warehouse bank has to take ownership of the note and deliver or sell it to be repaid.

ALTERNATIVES TO WAREHOUSING

Repurchase lines and commercial paper are two alternatives to warehouse lines for financing mortgage loans. With a repurchase line, the bank buys loans from the mortgage banker, who agrees to repurchase the loans at a specified time and price in the future for delivery to an investor. In contrast, commercial paper is a short-term, fixed-rate debt instrument issued by commercial banks. The paper is usually secured in some manner, ultimately by the mortgage loans. When interest rates on commercial paper are lower than the prime rate, it is a viable funding alternative.

Following closing and warehousing, the loans are shipped to the investor for review and purchase.

SHIPPING AND DELIVERY   **8**

The mortgage banker has two options once a loan closes: to place the loan in portfolio and earn interest on the loan for the length of its term, or to sell the loan in the secondary market and deliver it to an investor.

If the mortgage banker chooses to place the mortgage loan in its portfolio, which is rarely the case, shipping, delivery and warehousing are unnecessary. The mortgage banker need only set up the loan in its loan administration system and begin to service the loan for its term. In such a situation, the mortgage banker bears all of the interest rate and prepayment risk for that loan.

If the mortgage banker decides to sell the loan, the shipping department becomes involved. Since shipping consummates the loan process, activities performed by the origination, processing, underwriting and closing departments affect the quality of the loan product the shipping department will ultimately handle.

Shipping is the preparation, packaging and delivery of loan documents to an investor according to the terms of the commitment. Investor commitments require loan delivery by a specified date and according to stated investor requirements.

- Shipping functions include:

- matching loans with investor commitments,

- checking loan files for completeness,

- making copies of loan file documents,

- preparing transmittal documents,

- making physical or automated delivery of loan files and

- meeting delivery dates as stated in investor commitments.

INVESTOR COMMITMENTS

Each investor commitment carries such terms as commitment fee, total dollar volume of loans, interest rate, price, loan type and term, documentation requirements, and delivery date. The commitment spells out investor requirements for shipping and delivery; therefore, shipping personnel must follow the commitment to the letter.

The shipping department is involved with the investor commitment from the time negotiations begin between the marketing department and the investor until delivery of all loan documentation is completed. Representatives from origination, processing, underwriting, closing and shipping and delivery also must have input into the terms of the commitment. In doing so, all departments are aware of commitment specifics that affect their areas, and are accountable to meeting expectations. An investor commitment normally runs for a particular number of days or for a particular volume of loans — whichever comes first. An automated tickler file or systems matrix is employed to keep track of upcoming commitment expirations and delivery dates.

SHIPPING DUTIES

Shipping responsibilities vary from company to company, depending on the company's size and organization. In a small company, shipping may be simply packaging loans for delivery. In a large company, shipping may include loan inventory control, packaging and some marketing functions.

Typically, the shipper is continually in the process of filling investor and pool commitments, as directed by marketing. To fill pools, the shipper takes closed loans from a loan inventory report to determine what is available to fill the commitment. The loans must meet the terms of the commitment for yield, maturity, type and location of property, mortgage limits, mortgage term, mortgage insurance, mortgage instruments and LTV ratio.

Most loans that are closed to fill whole-loan investor commitments are already marked specifically for that commitment by the time the file reaches shipping. The loan file for each acceptable loan is then verified for the appropriate documentation. If the loan has just closed, some documents may be missing. The deed and mortgage, for example, will be unavailable while they are being recorded. Incomplete loan files can be delivered to the investor as long as missing items are documented and a follow-up system is in place to deliver promptly documents to the investor when received.

The shipper reviews a number of loan file details. The shipper must ensure that basic compliance documentation is in the file, and that each loan is the correct interest rate and product type. Loan amounts must also be verified. Normally there is a limit on each loan amount within the overall commitment, as well as a limit on the total dollar volume which may be applied to the commitment. LTV ratios and MI coverage have limits of acceptability as well.

Investors vary in their requirements for documentation. Some require only notification that the loans have been closed and insured or guaranteed. Others require that the entire loan file be forwarded to them. Loans sold servicing-retained transfer only minimal documentation, with the balance of the loan file retained by the servicing lender. Loans sold servicing-released require complete loan files to be transferred.

For each loan, the shipper must endorse the mortgage note and prepare the assignment of mortgage. The shipper must make sure all documents are executed, sealed and stamped as required. All originals and copies must be assembled in a specified order. If a file is being shipped to an investor, the shipper makes copies of the documents to satisfy the mortgage banker's internal auditors.

The shipper prepares the investor transmittal which lists the loans included in the package and where the purchase funds are being transmitted. If the loans are

to be pooled and converted into MBS, the shipper also prepares pool documents.

Delivery of the loans can be automated or physical. Fannie Mae and Freddie Mac have their own automated delivery systems — MORNET and MIDANET. These systems help delivery personnel work efficiently and accurately to avoid delivery delays. Ginnie Mae and most private investors require physical delivery.

As a quality control measure, some investors require final certification to verify that all documents, which may at one time have been outstanding, are in the loan file. Other investors occasionally audit their files to ensure commitment requirements are being met. Any problems uncovered may result in the lender repurchasing the offending loan(s). Repurchases harm the mortgage banker's reputation and are a serious financial burden.

Once a loan is delivered servicing-released, the borrower deals directly with the purchasing lender. If the loan is delivered servicing-retained, the borrower will make payments to the same lender who originated the loan.

LOAN ADMINISTRATION 9

Loan administration involves the collection of monthly mortgage payments from borrowers, the remittance of the appropriate portions of those payments to investors and the administration of escrows for the payment of property taxes, hazard insurance premiums and mortgage insurance premiums. Simply stated, loan administration consists of the administrative tasks necessary to manage closed loans.

The loan administration function is vital to a mortgage banking firm because it makes the largest contribution to net income. Mortgage companies that do not service must make up the income difference by collecting servicing-release premiums (SRPs) from purchasing lenders. These SRPs represent the present value of anticipated servicing revenue for that loan. While many investors insist on doing their own servicing as a condition of doing business, where the originator has a choice, the decision to service is

driven by that originator's profit strategy. Origination specialists (mortgage brokers) prefer to earn income quickly from origination fees and SRPs, while servicers (full-service mortgage bankers) prefer to build a profitable servicing portfolio over a longer period of time.

All of a traditional mortgage banker's activities are geared toward building the servicing portfolio. Loan administration functions include:

- setting up loan files,

- collecting and monitoring mortgage payments,

- responding quickly to customer inquiries,

- administering escrows,

- investor accounting and

- managing delinquencies and foreclosures.

LOAN ADMINISTRATION INCOME

Income from loan administration comes from servicing fees, ancillary fees, float and the sale of related services.

Servicing fees are normally 25–44 basis points (.25%–.44%) charged on the outstanding balance of the loan and collected monthly. The actual fee charged is regulated by the investor according to loan type. While this base fee appears small on a loan-by-loan basis, the total income on a large portfolio is significant and represents by far the mortgage banker's largest source of income.

Managing cost is the servicer's key to turning an impressive profit. Large mortgage servicers can take advantage of significant economies of scale only as long as they maintain productive and efficient operations — particularly in the delinquency and foreclosure areas. A large portfolio can be a disadvantage if it is not sufficiently diversified and well-managed.

Ancillary fees include late payments charges, assumption fees, discharge fees, bad check fees and prepayment penalties. Applicable fees are disclosed with the terms of each note. Charges may be invoked when special borrower services are required or when the borrower fails to pay the note as promised.

Float is earned from timing delays. Such delays occur between the date of receipt of mortgage payments from borrowers and the deadline date for remittance of a portion of those same payments to investors. When large loan balances are involved, float of 10–15 days can produce sizable earnings for the mortgage banker.

Many mortgage bankers use their servicing customer base to sell *related services* such as insurance, affiliated credit cards or consumer loans. Since these customers are already familiar with the mortgage banker's service capabilities, they may be more willing to extend their business relationship.

SERVICING AGREEMENT

A servicing agreement or contract outlines the servicing tasks an investor desires of the servicer. In addition to the traditional duties of receiving and remitting payments, the contract also specifies the servicer's duty to perform any activity necessary to protect the investor's security interest, including collection and foreclosure activities. The servicing agreement normally runs for the life of the loans or until terminated by the investor.

Mortgage bankers with origination volumes insufficient to support a servicing operation may opt to use a subservicer until they can build their servicing portfolio. In this case, the servicing agreement may contain an option to pull servicing when a stated mortgage volume is obtained.

LOAN FILE SETUP

New loans are set up on an automated servicing system shortly after closing. In the case of servicing purchased from another company, new loans are set up as soon as possible prior to the effective date of the transfer (first payment due) from the old servicer or originator. A supply of mortgage payment coupons should be generated and mailed to the borrower at this stage, along with an explanatory letter. The letter generally supplies information about the company and explains how to make payments. An amortization schedule and escrow statement may also be sent out at this stage.

MORTGAGE LOAN PAYMENTS

Mortgage loan payments consist of three components: principal, interest and escrow. Principal payments reduce the original loan and increase the borrower's equity in the property. Interest payments represent the investor's return for loaning funds. Finally, escrow payments protect the property as security for the mortgage.

Mortgage payments are collected for processing through a bank lock box. Payments are initially deposited into a clearing account. For mortgage bankers with large portfolios, the bank lock box will transmit transaction detail to the servicer's computer and update payment information on the borrower's account. Additionally, the servicer's computer software will generate reports and information

to transmit the payments electronically from the lock box account into the investor's custodial account. For mortgage bankers with small portfolios, the movement of funds from the lock box to custodial accounts is generally accomplished via PC modems.

Prepayments occur whenever a borrower pays off all or a portion of the obligation early. At payoff, the servicer prepares and records a satisfaction of mortgage, cancels the mortgage note and makes an escrow refund to the borrower. The investor is notified of the payoff.

ESCROWS

Escrows collected as a part of the borrower's monthly payment are accumulated for the payment of hazard insurance premiums, property taxes and other items when they come due. The hazard insurance policy ensures that if the property suffers a physical loss from wind, fire or other sources, it will be restored to its present condition. The property taxes, if not paid, can result in a lien on the property superior to the mortgage banker's claim.

In some cases, the escrow requirements may be waived by the lender. This is sometimes the case if the mortgage has a low LTV ratio, for example, below 80 percent. However, the lender still is obligated to follow up with each borrower to obtain evidence of insurance and property tax payment for the loan file.

Mortgage bankers analyze the adequacy of each borrower's escrow account, either annually or on an ongoing basis to avoid shortages and overages. Shortages occur when there is insufficient escrow accumulated to make a required payment. Overages occur when there is too much escrow accumulated. When a shortage occurs, the mortgage banker generally will advance the required funds to pay the item, and require repayment from the borrower over a 12-month period. Overages over and above the limits set by RESPA are refunded to the borrower. The monthly escrow payment is adjusted to compensate for overages and shortages whenever necessary. The payment of interest on these escrow accounts is governed by state law.

CUSTOMER SERVICE

Quality service for borrowers and investors is as important in loan servicing as operational efficiencies. A reputation for good service increases investor business and customer satisfaction.

Customer service representatives handle customer inquiries concerning assumptions, payoffs, transfers, partial releases, escrow payments, ARM conversion rates, etc. Many large servicers employ computerized tracking systems to monitor and respond efficiently to customer inquiries.

INVESTOR ACCOUNTING

An accounting of cash activity within the servicing operation is reported monthly to investors. In addition, a check or bank wire that distributes principal and interest less servicing fees for each loan is disbursed to the investor who purchased that loan. Depending on the servicing agreement and the type of remittance commitment the investor and servicer have agreed upon, the servicer may be responsible for paying the investor principal and interest regardless of whether they have been received. This particular kind of agreement gives the servicer a much broader base of investor capital to lend, and motivates the servicer to cure delinquencies quickly — since advances represent a major cost item.

DELINQUENCIES AND FORECLOSURES

Delinquencies are late-paying or nonpaying accounts. The further a borrower falls behind in making monthly payments, the more attention the servicer must give to collecting the account. Late-paying and nonpaying loans cost money in collection expenses and lost revenues. Investors look closely at delinquency ratios when choosing a mortgage servicer.

A loan delinquent beyond 30 days prompts the servicer's inquiry into the reason(s) for the delinquency. A phone call ascertains the borrower's ability and willingness to bring the loan current. At this point, the servicer may accelerate the entire debt or work out a payment plan. If a resolution cannot be found, the servicer may have to begin foreclosure proceedings.

An acceleration of the debt requires the outstanding mortgage balance to be paid immediately. In most cases, the borrower will be unable to retire the debt in this manner.

A workout allows the borrower to bring the debt current by restructuring payments. This is a viable cure because the lender does not have to take possession of the property, and the borrower does not lose any equity in the home. This cure requires thecooperation of the insuring/guaranteeing agency or MI and the investor.

A foreclosure is a legal proceeding in which the mortgaged property is given to the servicer who in turn sells the property in an effort to retire the mortgage debt. It is normally used only as a last resort. Despite the fact that most of a mortgage banker's loans are insured for just this purpose, foreclosure is a costly procedure that is avoided whenever possible.